Navigating the AI Frontier

I0407100

Thriving in the Business Evolution

Richard stones

Table of contents

I. Introduction

In a world where technology evolves at an unprecedented pace, the rise of artificial intelligence (AI) stands as one of the most influential trends impacting our industries, economies, and societies. The birth of the AI era signals a dramatic transformation in how businesses operate, innovate, and connect with their customers. Welcome to "Navigating the AI Frontier: Thriving in the Business Evolution," a detailed analysis of AI's impact on the modern business landscape.

As we stand on the cusp of this technological transformation, organizations across the globe are presented with both great opportunity and significant challenges. AI, formerly relegated to science fiction, has fast converted into reality, weaving its powers into every element of our existence. From personalized consumer experiences to predictive analytics, AI has the ability to restructure sectors, reinvent job positions, and radically shift how we approach business strategy.

This book is your guide to not just surviving, but thriving, in this new age of corporate evolution. We'll go into the essential principles of AI, demystifying complicated topics and offering a solid basis for comprehending its complexity. With clarity and simplicity, we'll cover the journey from narrow to general intelligence, unveiling the numerous shapes AI takes and the opportunities each brings.

Our adventure continues as we discuss the essentials of preparing for the AI revolution. How do you assess your organization's readiness for AI integration? What actions can you take to establish a robust AI-ready infrastructure? Beyond technology, we'll reveal the vital role of establishing an innovation-driven culture that accepts change and supports AI literacy.

The heart of this book is in the stories of transformation. Through specific chapters, we'll look into areas that AI is reshaping, from delivering unparalleled customer experiences to redefining how we make and distribute goods. Healthcare, banking, and many other areas are on the edge of revolutionary change, driven by AI-powered insights and solutions.

However, the route to success in the AI era is not without its hurdles. Crafting a strategic strategy, negotiating ethical considerations, and ensuring a seamless implementation are all crucial aspects that demand our attention. We'll analyze real-world case studies that emphasize both achievements and setbacks, providing vital insights for your own AI journey.

Finally, we glimpse into the future. The AI frontier includes cutting-edge technologies and new opportunities. As we stare ahead, we'll find new themes that will shape the landscape in the next few years. Moreover, we'll address a question that looms large in this AI revolution: How will humans interact with AI in the workforce of tomorrow?

As you embark on this adventure through "Navigating the AI Frontier," remember that you're not only a passive observer; you're an active player in creating your organization's fate in the age of AI. Together, we'll delve into the complexity, embrace the promise, and equip you with the insights you need to not only navigate, but thrive, in the dynamic world of business evolution powered by artificial intelligence.

The Rise of Artificial Intelligence in Business

In the annals of scientific advancement, few inventions have aroused as much enthusiasm and curiosity as artificial intelligence (AI). Once restricted to the pages of science fiction, AI has migrated from futuristic speculation to real-world application, altering the entire fabric of company operations, strategies, and possibilities.

As we see this seismic turmoil, it's evident that AI has transcended its position as a mere tool and emerged as a driving force behind the transformation of industries. The corporate landscape is undergoing a revolution— one propelled by the unmatched powers of AI to analyze enormous datasets, make predictions, automate operations, and learn from experience.

We kick off on a journey to uncover the complex emergence of AI in business. We'll traverse the timeline that led us to this important crossroads, from the early conceptions of machine intelligence to the sophisticated algorithms and neural networks that underlie today's AI systems.

AI is not merely a technology advancement; it's a philosophical revolution in how we view corporate strategy. Organizations are no longer bound to old models; instead, they're embracing AI to acquire insights into customer behavior, streamline processes, and create novel goods and services.

But the rise of AI isn't without its problems and challenges. How does the rapid development of AI affect job roles and labor dynamics? What ethical considerations arise when algorithms make decisions on our behalf? In investigating these issues, we're reminded that with tremendous power comes great responsibility.

The journey towards the AI age is marked by both optimism and caution. AI is set to boost our capabilities, unlock new channels of growth, and push the boundaries of what's attainable. Yet, it also involves careful navigation—a balance between innovation and ethics, between advancement and preservation.

As we explore into the revolutionary landscape of AI in business, realize that the journey is not simply one of technology but of deep change. It's a journey that will question our views of labor, creativity, and even the definition of intelligence itself. Join us as we navigate the growth of artificial intelligence and delve into the huge opportunities it presents to transform the way we do business.

Embracing Change: The Imperative for AI Adoption

The capacity to adapt isn't just a benefit in the dynamic corporate world—it's a requirement. This is especially true in the field of artificial intelligence (AI), where embracing change is not just a wise strategic move but also a necessity for continued relevance and expansion.

We go deeply into the nature of change as it relates to the adoption of AI in this book. Businesses that fight the fast currents of technological advancement run the risk of being cast adrift in a sea of rivals that have successfully used AI to their advantage.

We start by analyzing the justifications for the necessity of adopting AI. Personalized experiences are in high demand, and the exponential growth of data has ushered in a new era where manual analysis and decision-making are inadequate. AI has emerged as the key to gaining access to the insights that fuel innovation and competition because of its ability to analyse data at a size and pace that are unimaginable to humans.

But adopting AI requires a culture shift rather than merely a strategic decision. We discuss the mindset necessary to successfully navigate this transformational path, touching on the desire to challenge the status quo, the openness to experimentation, and the understanding that AI is not a single event but rather an ongoing evolution.

Importantly, this book addresses the worries and apprehensions that the adoption of AI may cause. After all, change can be uncomfortable. We dispel popular myths and shed light on the idea that artificial intelligence (AI) isn't a force to replace people but to enhance their capabilities—to raise us from regular jobs and free us to concentrate on higher-order thinking and creativity.

The call for AI adoption is resonating across industries, from startups to well-established businesses. Stories of people who have accepted change and benefited from it serve as motivation. We demonstrate the real advantages that AI integration can bring—increased productivity, better decision-making, greater customer experiences, and the ability to create novel business models—through fascinating case studies.

Finally, we throw down the challenge. The terrain is changing, and those who opt to adapt instead than resist will determine the course of success. The need for AI adoption goes beyond technology; it is a call to embrace change as a driver of advancement and to reorient organizational priorities toward a time when success will depend on creativity.

As you progress through this project, keep in mind that the need for AI adoption isn't just a suggestion; **it's a strong demand that forces companies to flourish in the face of unheard-of upheaval.**

Chapter 1

Understanding AI Basics

The ability to comprehend the foundational ideas of AI is now essential rather than a luxury. This chapter serves as your introduction to the complex world of artificial intelligence (AI), explaining its fundamental concepts and demystifying the language that frequently accompanies it.

To start, let's look at what AI really is, what it isn't, and how it varies from conventional computing. We provide insight into the principles that allow AI systems to imitate human cognitive functions by exploring the theoretical underpinnings of machine learning and neural networks.

Next, we explore the diversity of AI, from narrow AI—specialized systems that excel at a restricted range of tasks—to the more elusive broad AI, where robots are capable of doing any intellectual task that a human can on their own. The scope of AI's potential and the repercussions of moving along this spectrum are shown by this voyage.

As we immerse ourselves in the world of AI, we come across crucial words and ideas that act as the foundation for comprehension. In order to help you communicate fluently in this revolutionary field, we decode the language of AI, covering everything from algorithms and training data to supervised and unsupervised learning.

The course of AI is determined not only by its capabilities but also by the ethical issues that come with its development. In order to keep us aware of the obligations involved in the creation and use of AI as we learn more about it, this chapter addresses issues of bias, accountability, and transparency.

This chapter offers the foundation of AI literacy, helping both corporate leaders navigate the landscape of AI and curious minds eager to understand the technological marvels altering our world. We enable you to not only comprehend AI but also to interact with it meaningfully—a step that serves as the key to opening up its limitless potential—through clarity, insights, and relatable examples.

Demystifying AI: Concepts and Terminology

What exactly is AI?

Artificial intelligence (AI) is the term used to describe how machines, particularly computer systems, simulate human intelligence processes. Learning, thinking, solving problems, perception, and language comprehension are some of these processes. Artificial intelligence (AI) systems are designed to replicate human cognitive processes so they can carry out tasks that normally require human intelligence.

Discoveries and AI Evolution:

Though AI has existed since the beginning of time, it was not until the middle of the 20th century that it received official acknowledgment. At the Dartmouth Workshop, the phrase "artificial intelligence" was first used in 1956, which launched the academic field of AI study. Rule-based systems gave way to more complex techniques like machine learning and neural networks as AI developed through time.

The benefits of AI

A number of advantages that AI provides include:

Automation: AI can automate labor-intensive, repetitive operations to improve productivity and lower human error.

Data analysis: AI is capable of fast processing and analyzing big datasets to uncover insightful patterns.

Personalization: AI makes it possible for experiences to be tailored to a user's tastes and behavior.

AI facilitates decision-making by offering data-driven suggestions and forecasts.

AI promotes innovation by making it possible to develop new goods, services, and business strategies.

The Transformational Effect of AI

AI is changing the world in a number of ways, including:

Healthcare: AI helps with medication discovery, medical diagnostics, and individualized treatment programs.

Production: AI-driven automation improves productivity, quality assurance, and preventive maintenance.

Finance: In the financial industry, AI improves trading, risk assessment, fraud detection, and customer service.

Retail: AI makes it possible to manage inventories, engage customers, and personalize marketing.

Predictive maintenance and self-driving automobiles are transforming the transportation sector.

Education: AI automates administrative tasks and enables tailored learning experiences.

Adoption and appeal:

The popularity of AI has grown significantly in recent years as a result of technological developments and increasing data accessibility. Across all sectors, companies are implementing AI to gain a competitive edge, simplify workflows, and improve consumer experiences.

Various AI types

Narrow AI (Weak AI): AI created and taught for a single purpose, such as translating languages or recognizing images.

General AI (Strong AI): AI has cognitive powers comparable to those of humans, able to comprehend, pick up new information, and reason about a variety of activities. General AI is still only a theory.

AI in the Workplace:

There are several many business uses for AI:

Chatbots and virtual assistants offer round-the-clock customer service.

Marketing: AI examines consumer information to develop specialized marketing efforts.

Supply Chain: AI enhances logistics, demand forecasting, and inventory control.

Sales: AI supports customer profiling, lead scoring, and sales forecasting.

AI streamlines candidate screening and raises staff involvement in HR and recruitment.

In conclusion, AI is a dynamic force that is transforming industries, streamlining procedures, and improving decision-making. Its growing popularity encourages innovation and gives businesses the resources they need to prosper in a world dominated by technology.

Several significant terms that are frequently used in artificial intelligence are outlined below:

Artificial intelligence (AI) is the computer modeling of cognitive functions like learning, reasoning, problem-solving, and decision-making that occur in humans.

Machine Learning (ML) is a subset of artificial intelligence that uses algorithms to let computers learn from data and get better over time.

Neural Networks: A collection of algorithms used for pattern recognition and machine learning tasks that are modeled after the structure of the human brain.

Deep learning is a kind of machine learning that makes use of neural networks with numerous layers and is frequently applied to challenging tasks like speech and picture recognition.

Algorithm: A detailed plan of steps that computers use to complete a task or address a challenge.

Data mining is the process of applying machine learning and artificial intelligence to uncover patterns and insights from huge databases.

The goal of the area of *natural language processing* (NLP) is to make it possible for computers to comprehend, analyze, and produce human language.

Computer vision is a branch of artificial intelligence that deals with teaching machines to comprehend and interpret visual data from the outside world, such as pictures and movies.

A type of machine learning known as *supervised learning* aims to learn the relationship between inputs and outputs by training the model using labeled data.

Unsupervised learning is a sort of machine learning where the model is trained on unlabeled data with the aim of identifying structures or patterns in the data.

A type of machine learning called *reinforcement learning* teaches an agent how to operate in a given environment in order to maximize a reward signal.

The act of choosing and modifying pertinent features (variables) from raw data to enhance the performance of machine learning models is known as **feature engineering.**

Bias and Fairness: The existence of systematic biases or faults in AI systems that may produce unfair results for particular populations.

Overfitting: When a machine learning model performs poorly on new, untrained data because it learned the training data too well.

When a machine learning model is too basic to detect the underlying patterns in the data and performs badly overall, this is known as **underfitting.**

Algorithmic bias is the unintentional prejudice introduced by biased training data or biased algorithms in AI systems.

The process of converting unstructured data into a form more suited to machine learning algorithms is known as **feature extraction.**

A form of machine learning problem called regression entails forecasting a continuous numerical value.

Data must be categorized into preset classes or labels in order to perform a classification operation.

Clustering is an unsupervised learning technique that groups comparable data elements according to their properties.

Ensemble learning is a method for enhancing overall predicting performance by combining various machine learning models.

Hyperparameters: Predetermined factors that have an impact on how machine learning algorithms behave.

Feature selection is the process of selecting a dataset's most pertinent features in order to enhance model performance and simplify it.

Gradient Descent: An optimization technique that iteratively modifies a model's parameters in order to reduce error.

Transfer learning is a method for starting a new task with little or no data by using a model that has already been trained.

The purpose of supervised classification, a form of supervised learning, is to classify data into distinct groups or categories.

Unsupervised Clustering is a branch of unsupervised learning in which data is clustered according to underlying patterns.

Convolutional neural networks (CNNs) are a particular kind of neural network created specifically for processing grid-like data, such as photographs.

A sort of neural network called a **recurrent neural network (RNN)** is made to handle sequential data, such as text or time-series data.

An example of a neural network system for creating new data instances that mimic an existing dataset is the generative adversarial network (GAN).

Often employed for customer service, a **Chatbot** is a conversational AI system that communicates with users using natural language.

Artificial Neural Network (ANN): A computational model used for machine learning that is based on the structure and operation of the human brain.

The balance between a model's aptitude for accurately fitting training data (low bias) and its capacity for generalization to fresh data (low variance).

Decision Tree: A tree-like structure that uses feature values to inform judgments during classification and regression tasks.

Random Forest: An ensemble learning technique that builds several decision trees and combines their forecasts for more precise outcomes.

Metrics used to assess the effectiveness of classification models, particularly in datasets with imbalances, are precision and recall.

Using a process known as "one-hot encoding," categorical data can be transformed into a binary matrix format that is appropriate for machine learning techniques.

A mathematical function that is frequently employed as an activation function in neural networks to add nonlinearity is the **sigmoid function.**

Loss Function: In machine learning models, a function that measures the discrepancy between anticipated and actual values.

A constant neuron called a **bias neuron** is introduced to neural network architectures to assist the model learn and take biases into consideration.

These terminologies cover a range of AI topics, from fundamental ideas to particular strategies and procedures. Learning these words can make it easier to comprehend the literature, conversations, and applications of AI.

Chapter 2

Preparing for the AI Journey

This chapter serves as your guide through the intricate process of preparing your organization for the exciting and transformative world of artificial intelligence.

We begin by assessing the readiness of your business for AI integration. What are your organization's strengths and gaps in terms of data availability, technological infrastructure, and human resources? This introspective exploration lays the foundation for a robust AI strategy.

Building an AI-ready infrastructure is a pivotal step in this journey. From data collection, storage, and preprocessing to selecting appropriate AI tools and platforms, every element forms a crucial piece of the puzzle. We delve into the intricacies of data, often referred to as the "fuel" of AI, and how to ensure its quality, relevance, and security.

Yet, the AI journey transcends technology—it's a cultural shift that demands fostering a culture of innovation and AI literacy. We delve into the mindset needed to embrace change, cultivate creativity, and empower employees to engage with AI as a transformative force.

Ethical considerations form an integral aspect of AI preparation. The power of AI brings responsibilities— addressing questions of fairness, accountability, and transparency is paramount. We explore the importance of embedding ethics in AI development and deployment to ensure that AI aligns with organizational values and societal expectations.

Throughout this chapter, we weave real-world examples of businesses that have navigated the AI journey successfully. These stories offer insights into challenges faced, strategies employed, and lessons learned, providing you with a roadmap to navigate the complexities of AI implementation.

As you embark on the preparatory phase of the AI journey, remember that it's more than just adopting new technology—it's about cultivating an ecosystem where technology, culture, and values align to drive innovation and growth. This chapter equips you with the knowledge and insights needed to prepare your organization for a future where AI isn't just a tool, but a transformative catalyst.

Few real-world examples of businesses that have successfully navigated the AI journey:

Netflix: The streaming giant employs AI to personalize recommendations for its users. The "Netflix Recommends" algorithm analyzes viewing habits and user preferences to suggest content that aligns with individual tastes, enhancing user engagement and retention.

Amazon: Amazon's AI-driven recommendation engine is a prime example of successful AI integration. The "Customers Who Bought This Also Bought" feature employs machine learning algorithms to analyze purchasing patterns and offer personalized product suggestions to users.

Google: Google's search engine utilizes AI algorithms, particularly the RankBrain algorithm, to interpret and understand the context of search queries. This enables more accurate search results and improves the user experience.

Tesla: Tesla's autonomous driving technology is built on AI and machine learning. The company collects vast amounts of data from its vehicles to continuously improve its self-driving capabilities and enhance safety features.

IBM Watson: IBM's AI platform, Watson, has been employed in various industries. For instance, in healthcare, Watson is used for diagnosing diseases and suggesting treatment options by analyzing vast amounts of medical literature and patient data.

Walmart: Walmart uses AI to optimize inventory management and supply chain operations. Machine learning algorithms predict demand patterns and ensure that stores are stocked with the right products at the right time.

Uber: Uber's platform relies heavily on AI for dynamic pricing, route optimization, and matching riders with drivers efficiently. The company's algorithms consider factors like traffic conditions and rider demand to optimize ride-sharing experiences.

Airbnb: Airbnb employs AI to improve its user experience. The platform uses AI to analyze user preferences and behaviors, providing personalized accommodation recommendations and optimizing search results.

Coca-Cola: Coca-Cola uses AI-powered vending machines that adjust their product offerings based on factors such as weather, time of day, and customer demographics. This customization enhances customer satisfaction.

Starbucks: Starbucks utilizes AI for its mobile app's order and payment features. The app learns customer preferences and suggests customized drinks and food items, streamlining the ordering process.

These examples highlight the diverse applications of AI across various industries, from entertainment and e-commerce to transportation and hospitality. Successful AI implementation involves leveraging data, adopting the right algorithms, and focusing on enhancing customer experiences, operational efficiency, and innovation.

Assessing Your Business Readiness for AI Integration

Assessing readiness for AI integration in your specific business sector involves a tailored approach. Here's a sector-specific guide to help you assess your readiness for AI in your business:

Identify Key Business Processes:

Identify the core business processes in your sector that could benefit from AI. These could include customer service, supply chain management, marketing, product development, etc.

Gather Industry Insights:

Research how AI is being used in your sector. Look for case studies and success stories of businesses similar to yours that have integrated AI effectively.

Define Your AI Goals:

Determine the specific goals you want to achieve with AI in your sector. Whether it's improving efficiency, personalizing customer experiences, or optimizing decision-making, align AI goals with your sector's needs.

Assess Data Availability:

Evaluate the availability of relevant and high-quality data in your sector. Data is crucial for AI, so assess whether you have access to the data needed to train AI models for your sector-specific use cases.

Evaluate Technology Infrastructure:

Examine your sector's existing technology infrastructure. Does it support AI implementation? Assess factors like computing power, software tools, and compatibility with AI platforms.

Understand Regulatory and Ethical Considerations:

Different sectors have varying regulatory frameworks and ethical considerations. Evaluate how AI integration might impact compliance and ethical standards in your sector.

Analyzing Workforce Skills:

Assess the skills of your workforce in your sector. Do your employees have the necessary skills to work with AI? Identify skill gaps and consider training programs or hiring AI professionals.

Industry-Specific Challenges:

Consider the unique challenges that your sector might face in adopting AI. These could include sector-specific data complexities, privacy concerns, or customer expectations.

Cost-Benefit Analysis:

Conduct a cost-benefit analysis specific to your sector. Assess the potential ROI of integrating AI against the costs involved in terms of technology upgrades, training, and implementation.

Pilot Projects:

Consider starting with small-scale AI pilot projects in your sector. These projects can help you test the waters, learn from initial experiences, and gather insights before full-scale implementation.

Engage Industry Experts:

Consult with experts or consultants who have experience in AI adoption within your sector. They can provide insights and guidance tailored to your industry's nuances.

Remember that assessing readiness for AI in your business sector is an ongoing process. As technology, regulations, and market dynamics evolve, continue to adapt your strategy to ensure successful AI integration in your sector.

Building an AI-Ready Infrastructure: Data, Tools, and Resources

Construction of an infrastructure that is AI-ready demands careful design and implementation. The following advice will help you build a strong foundation for AI integration:

Clearly identify your objectives and the issues you hope to address with AI. You may better connect your infrastructure-building activities with your company objectives with this insight.

Analyze Data Availability: Consider the data you already have in relation to your AI objectives. Recognize any gaps and think about what extra information may be required for precise model training.

Make sure your data is accurate, relevant, and of high quality. AI models may become unreliable as a result of bad data. Spend money on preparation, validation, and data cleansing.

Establishing strong data security and privacy protections is important. Protect sensitive consumer data and abide with applicable data protection laws.

Select the Correct Tools: Choose AI platforms and technologies that are in line with the objectives and needs of your firm. Think on things like usability, integration potential, and scalability.

Utilize Cloud Solutions: Cloud platforms provide scalable, adaptable, and affordable AI solutions. Think about AI cloud-based services that can make managing infrastructure easier.eg:

Upskill your employees with AI concepts, tools, and practices by investing in training. Workshops, certificates, and training courses can enable your staff to use AI productively.

Encourage cross-functional cooperation amongst data scientists, engineers, subject matter experts, and business stakeholders. A multidisciplinary approach guarantees a thorough comprehension of AI use cases.

Start Small: To test and validate your AI infrastructure, start with small pilot projects. Prior to full-scale implementation, starting small enables you to learn from early experiences and make improvements.

Ethics: Establish moral standards for the use of AI. Make sure your AI procedures follow the values of accountability, openness, and justice.

AI infrastructure monitoring and improvement are constant tasks. To increase precision and relevance, keep an eye on model performance, get input, and iterate.

Scale your AI endeavors gradually as you gain confidence and experience. Initially, avoid going overboard; instead, concentrate on progressively increasing the use of AI.

Stay Current: AI technology is advancing quickly. Keep up with the most recent developments, trends, and best practices to keep your infrastructure up to date.

Consider talking with outside AI specialists or working with AI solution suppliers. Their knowledge can make the infrastructure-building process more efficient.

User-Centric Approach: When developing your infrastructure, keep the end user in mind. User experiences should be improved by AI solutions, which should also tackle current issues.

Measurable Metrics: Establish Key performance indicators (KPI) to gauge the accomplishment of your AI activities. Use these indicators to measure progress on a regular basis.

Feedback Loop: Create a feedback loop with stakeholders and users. Their perspectives can offer insightful data that will help you improve and optimize your AI architecture.

Build your AI infrastructure with a long-term perspective as your long-term strategy. Think about how it fits into the larger digital transformation strategy of your company.

By implementing these suggestions, you can build an infrastructure that is prepared for AI, positioning your business for effective innovation and integration into the AI ecosystem.

How to Cultivate a Culture of Innovation and AI Literacy

Cultivating a culture of innovation and AI literacy within your organization is essential for successful AI integration. Here are steps you can take to foster such a culture:

Leadership Buy-In:

Leadership support is crucial for fostering a culture of innovation. Leaders should champion AI initiatives, allocate resources, and communicate the importance of innovation to the entire organization.

Clear Vision and Strategy:

Develop a clear vision for how AI can drive innovation and business growth. Create a strategic roadmap that outlines the goals, benefits, and steps for AI integration.

Educational Initiatives:

Offer training programs and workshops on AI fundamentals for employees at all levels. These initiatives can range from basic awareness sessions to in-depth technical training.

Internal Communication:

Regularly communicate the value of AI and its potential impact on the organization. Highlight success stories, case studies, and industry trends to inspire and educate employees.

Cross-Functional Collaboration:

Encourage collaboration across departments. Cross-functional teams can bring diverse perspectives to AI projects and spark innovative ideas.

Innovation Challenges:

Organize innovation challenges or hackathons focused on AI. These events provide employees with opportunities to brainstorm and develop AI-driven solutions.

Safe Experimentation:

Create a safe environment for experimentation. Encourage employees to explore AI concepts, test hypotheses, and learn from failures without fear of repercussions.

Resource Allocation:

Allocate time, budget, and resources for innovation projects. Dedicate a portion of working hours to explore new ideas and technologies.

Recognition and Rewards:

Recognize and reward employees who contribute innovative ideas or actively participate in AI initiatives. Publicly acknowledge their efforts and outcomes.

Open Innovation Channels:

Establish channels for employees to share their ideas, suggestions, and concerns related to AI. This can include suggestion boxes, online platforms, or regular innovation meetings.

External Learning Opportunities:

Encourage employees to attend AI conferences, workshops, and webinars. Exposure to external learning opportunities can expand their knowledge and inspire new ideas.

Mentorship and Coaching:

Pair employees interested in AI with experienced mentors or coaches. This mentorship can provide guidance, answer questions, and offer insights from real-world experiences.

Fail Fast Mentality:

Promote a "fail fast, learn faster" mindset. Encourage employees to view failures as learning experiences and iterate on their ideas based on feedback.

Innovation Labs:

Establish dedicated spaces or labs where employees can collaborate, experiment, and brainstorm innovative AI solutions.

Long-Term Commitment:

Cultivating a culture of innovation and AI literacy is a long-term endeavor. Consistently reinforce these principles to embed them into the organizational DNA.

Celebrate Successes:

Celebrate both small and significant successes in AI integration. Highlight the positive impact on the organization, customers, and employees.

Chapter 3

Ai in action

The realm of artificial intelligence transcends theory, manifesting its transformative potential across a multitude of industries and applications. This chapter is your window into the real-world impact of AI, offering a panoramic view of how this technology is reshaping industries, augmenting processes, and revolutionizing customer experiences.

Healthcare Revolution:

Explore how AI is revolutionizing healthcare. From diagnosing diseases through medical imaging to predicting patient outcomes, AI-driven insights are enhancing diagnostic accuracy and enabling personalized treatment plans.

Retail Transformation:

Witness the transformation of the retail landscape. AI is powering recommendation engines, optimizing supply chains, and enabling dynamic pricing strategies that adapt to market dynamics in real-time.

Financial Services Reinvention:

Dive into the reimagined financial services sector. AI is driving fraud detection, automating trading, and enabling personalized financial advice, creating a more secure and customer-centric financial ecosystem.

Manufacturing Evolution:

Uncover the evolution of manufacturing. AI-driven predictive maintenance, quality control, and process optimization are driving efficiency, reducing downtime, and minimizing defects.

Transportation Revolution:

Embark on a journey through the transportation revolution. Self-driving cars, smart traffic management, and predictive maintenance are reshaping the way we move, enhancing safety and efficiency.

Media and Entertainment Innovation:

Experience the innovation in media and entertainment. AI-powered content recommendation, video analysis, and personalized marketing are redefining how content is created, distributed, and consumed.

Energy and Utilities Enhancement:

Witness the enhancement of energy and utilities. AI-driven demand forecasting, energy optimization, and predictive maintenance are fostering sustainability and efficiency.

Agriculture Advancement:

Explore the advancement of agriculture. AI-powered precision farming, crop monitoring, and pest detection are optimizing yields and promoting sustainable agricultural practices.

Education Transformation:

Discover the transformation in education. AI-driven personalized learning, intelligent tutoring, and analytics are reshaping how students learn and educators teach.

Customer Service Evolution:

Witness the evolution of customer service. Chatbots, virtual assistants, and sentiment analysis are revolutionizing customer interactions, providing round-the-clock support.

Real-world instances of AI applications in various industries:

As earlier stated, Ai plays a huge role in various industries and some are also listed below

Healthcare:

Medical Imaging Analysis: AI algorithms analyze medical images like X-rays and MRIs to aid radiologists in detecting diseases like cancer and identifying anomalies.

Drug Discovery: AI models process large datasets to identify potential drug candidates and predict their effectiveness in treating diseases.

Personalized Treatment Plans: AI analyzes patient data to create personalized treatment plans based on factors like genetics and medical history.

Retail:

Recommendation Systems: AI-powered recommendation engines suggest products to customers based on their browsing history and purchase patterns.

Dynamic Pricing: AI algorithms analyze market demand and competitor pricing to adjust product prices in real-time for optimal sales and revenue.

Inventory Management: AI predicts demand patterns and optimizes inventory levels to prevent stockouts and reduce excess inventory costs.

Manufacturing:

Predictive Maintenance: AI monitors equipment data to predict maintenance needs, reducing downtime and increasing operational efficiency.

Quality Control: AI-driven vision systems identify defects in products during the manufacturing process, improving product quality.

Process Optimization: AI optimizes manufacturing processes by analyzing data and adjusting variables for maximum efficiency.

Transportation:

Self-Driving Vehicles: AI powers autonomous vehicles, enabling them to navigate and make decisions without human intervention.

Traffic Management: AI analyzes real-time traffic data to optimize traffic signal timings, reducing congestion and improving traffic flow.

Predictive Maintenance for Vehicles: AI monitors vehicle data to predict maintenance needs, reducing breakdowns and increasing safety.

Energy and Utilities:

Energy Consumption Optimization: AI analyzes energy consumption patterns to optimize energy usage, reduce costs, and minimize environmental impact.

Predictive Maintenance for Utilities: AI predicts equipment failures in utility infrastructure, enabling proactive maintenance and preventing service disruptions.

Renewable Energy Forecasting: AI predicts renewable energy production based on weather patterns, optimizing energy distribution.

Education:

Personalized Learning: AI adapts learning materials and pace to individual student needs, enhancing engagement and comprehension.

Intelligent Tutoring: AI-powered virtual tutors provide real-time assistance to students, helping them understand complex concepts.

Assessment Automation: AI automates grading and assessment, providing teachers with more time for personalized instruction.

Customer Service:

Chatbots and Virtual Assistants: AI-powered chatbots handle customer queries 24/7, providing quick responses and improving customer satisfaction.

Sentiment Analysis: AI analyzes customer feedback and social media data to gauge customer sentiment and identify areas for improvement.

Call Center Optimization: AI analyzes call center interactions to improve call routing, agent performance, and customer interactions.

These real-world examples showcase the diverse ways in which AI is transforming industries and enhancing various aspects of business operations and customer experiences.

Revolutionizing Manufacturing and Supply Chain Management

The role of AI in revolutionizing manufacturing and supply chain management is transformative, as it brings a new level of intelligence, efficiency, and agility to these sectors. Here are some key roles that AI plays in this revolution:

Predictive Maintenance: AI analyzes data from sensors and equipment to predict when machines are likely to fail. This enables proactive maintenance, reduces unplanned downtime, and extends equipment lifespan.

Optimized Production: AI analyzes real-time production data to identify bottlenecks, inefficiencies, and process improvements. It helps streamline production processes, reduce waste, and enhance overall efficiency.

Quality Assurance: AI-driven computer vision systems inspect products with precision, detecting defects and variations that might be missed by human inspectors. This ensures higher product quality and consistency.

Inventory Management: AI uses historical data, sales trends, and external factors to predict demand accurately.

This optimizes inventory levels, reduces excess stock, and prevents stockouts.

Supply Chain Agility: AI analyzes market trends, economic indicators, and customer behavior to enhance supply chain responsiveness. It helps businesses adapt quickly to changes in demand, supply, and market conditions.

Demand Forecasting: AI improves demand forecasting accuracy by analyzing large datasets and identifying patterns. This enables companies to align production schedules with actual demand and reduce overproduction.

Supplier Relationship Enhancement: AI analyzes supplier data, performance metrics, and external factors to make informed decisions about supplier selection, collaboration, and risk management.

Risk Management: AI simulates various scenarios to assess potential disruptions and risks in the supply chain. It helps companies develop strategies to mitigate risks and enhance supply chain resilience.

Real-Time Insights: AI-powered analytics provide real-time visibility into production processes, inventory levels, and supply chain operations. This enables quick decision-making and performance optimization.

Resource Optimization: AI analyzes resource consumption patterns to optimize energy usage, reduce waste, and promote sustainable practices in manufacturing and supply chain operations.

Automation and Robotics: AI-driven robots and automated systems are increasingly used in manufacturing for tasks like assembly, packaging, and material handling, leading to increased efficiency and accuracy.

Collaborative Robots (Cobots): AI-powered cobots work alongside human workers, enhancing safety and efficiency in manufacturing processes.

Customization and Personalization: AI enables mass customization by analyzing customer preferences and tailoring products to individual needs, reducing the need for large inventories.

Sustainability Initiatives: AI helps identify areas where energy consumption and waste can be reduced, contributing to sustainable manufacturing practices.

Continuous Improvement: AI enables continuous monitoring and analysis of processes, helping manufacturers identify opportunities for improvement and innovation.

In essence, AI's role in manufacturing and supply chain management is to optimize processes, enhance decision-making, reduce costs, and increase responsiveness. By leveraging AI technologies, organizations can drive efficiency, quality, and innovation across their entire value chain.

AI in Healthcare: Enhancing Diagnostics and Treatment

Healthcare AI has advanced significantly, especially in terms of improving diagnostic and therapeutic procedures. Here are some ways that AI is revolutionizing certain fields:

1. Diagonistics

Medical Image Analysis: AI algorithms are capable of analyzing medical pictures such as X-rays, MRIs, and CT scans to help radiologists accurately identify abnormalities like tumors or fractures.

Histology and Pathology: AI assists pathologists in classifying and identifying cancer in tissue samples, minimizing human error and accelerating the diagnostic procedure.

Early Disease diagnosis: Artificial intelligence (AI) models can spot small patterns and signals in patient data, allowing for the early diagnosis of conditions like diabetic retinopathy, Alzheimer's, and some types of cancer.

2. Therapy:

Personalized Treatment Plans: Using analysis of big datasets, AI may create treatment plans that are specific to each patient's genetic make-up, medical history, and way of life.

Drug Discovery: AI greatly cuts the time and expense associated with drug discovery by foreseeing prospective drug candidates and simulating their interactions with biological systems.

AI-powered systems that evaluate medical records, clinical recommendations, and research publications provide therapy recommendations to help clinicians make well-informed treatment choices.

Robot-assisted surgery: To execute complex surgeries precisely and with the least amount of invasiveness and recuperation time, surgeons can use robotic devices led by AI.

3. Patient Care:

3. Remote Monitoring: AI-enabled wearables can track patients' vital signs continually, aiding in the management of chronic illnesses and warning medical professionals of any irregularities.

Virtual health assistants: AI-powered chatbots and virtual assistants can give patients advice on general health issues, reminders for their medications, and information about their diseases.

AI algorithms that use predictive analytics can foresee patient difficulties or worsening, enabling healthcare professionals to take preemptive action.

4. Data Insights and Analysis:

Utilization of Big Data: AI analyzes vast amounts of medical data to find insights and trends that human analysis could overlook, resulting in better diagnoses and treatments.

Clinical Research: AI aids in the selection of test subjects, the analysis of trial data, and even the forecasting of possible outcomes.

Healthcare Management: AI helps hospitals and healthcare organizations allocate resources, schedule staff more efficiently, and anticipate patient admissions.

Challenges and Things to Think About

Despite its promise, applying AI to healthcare presents a number of difficulties, including issues with data privacy, security, regulatory compliance, and potential biases in AI systems. Before mass deployment, it is essential to make sure that AI systems are open, accountable, and extensively validated.

Although AI's place in healthcare is still being developed, its influence on improving diagnosis and treatment cannot be denied. AI has the potential to change the healthcare sector, resulting in improved patient outcomes and more effective healthcare systems, as technology develops and ethical issues are addressed.

Some major breakthrough of Ai in Medicine or Healthcare

there have been several major breakthroughs in AI within the field of medicine and healthcare. Here are some notable examples:

IBM Watson for Oncology: IBM's Watson, a powerful AI platform, has been used in oncology to assist doctors in identifying personalized treatment options for cancer patients. By analyzing vast amounts of medical literature, clinical trial data, and patient records, Watson provides treatment recommendations that align with the latest research.

Google's DeepMind AlphaFold: DeepMind's AlphaFold is an AI system that predicts the 3D structures of proteins, a task critical for understanding diseases and developing new drugs. In 2020, AlphaFold made headlines by predicting protein structures with remarkable accuracy, potentially accelerating drug discovery and advancing our understanding of various diseases.

PathAI's Pathology Solutions: PathAI has developed AI-powered solutions for pathology, helping pathologists accurately analyze tissue samples and detect diseases such as cancer. Their technology enhances diagnostic accuracy and efficiency, enabling earlier disease detection and better patient outcomes.

FDA-approved AI Algorithms: In 2018, the U.S. Food and Drug Administration (FDA) approved the first AI algorithm, IDx-DR, capable of detecting diabetic retinopathy in retinal images without the need for a doctor's interpretation. This marked a significant step toward integrating AI into clinical decision-making.

Robot-Assisted Surgery: Companies like Intuitive Surgical have developed robots like the da Vinci Surgical System, which aid surgeons in performing minimally invasive procedures with greater precision. These systems translate the surgeon's hand movements into precise actions, reducing patient trauma and speeding up recovery times.

Detecting Skin Cancer: AI algorithms have been developed to analyze images of skin lesions and moles, helping dermatologists in early detection of skin cancer. Companies like DermDetect and MetaOptima's DermEngine use AI to assist in identifying potential malignancies.

Health Monitoring Wearables: Wearable devices like the Apple Watch and Fitbit use AI to monitor users' heart rates, sleep patterns, and physical activities. These devices can alert users and healthcare providers to irregularities, contributing to better management of chronic conditions.

Drug Discovery with BenevolentAI: BenevolentAI employs AI to sift through vast databases of medical research and scientific literature to identify potential drug candidates for various diseases. The platform's AI-driven predictions have the potential to expedite drug discovery processes.

COVID-19 Response: During the COVID-19 pandemic, AI was used to analyze medical imaging, genomic data, and clinical records to better understand the virus and develop diagnostic tools. AI also played a role in predicting disease spread and identifying potential drug treatments.

Personalized Medicine: AI has enabled the development of personalized treatment plans by analyzing genetic information, medical history, and other patient data. This approach tailors interventions to individual patients, optimizing outcomes and minimizing side effects.

These breakthroughs highlight the transformative potential of AI in medicine and healthcare. As AI technologies continue to advance, we can expect even more innovative applications that improve patient care, diagnostics, treatment, and overall healthcare processes.

Finance and Fintech: AI's Impact on Transactions and Security

AI has had a profound impact on the finance and fintech industries, revolutionizing the way transactions are conducted and enhancing security measures. Here's how AI has influenced these areas:

1. Transactions:

Algorithmic Trading: AI-powered algorithms analyze market data and execute trades at high speeds, optimizing investment strategies and capitalizing on market inefficiencies.

Predictive Analytics: AI models analyze historical data and real-time market trends to predict asset price movements, assisting traders and investors in making informed decisions.

Fraud Detection: AI systems monitor transactions for unusual patterns and behaviors, flagging potentially fraudulent activities in real-time to prevent financial losses.

Customer Service: Chatbots and virtual assistants powered by AI handle customer inquiries, streamline account management, and provide assistance with transactions.

2. Security:

Fraud Prevention: AI analyzes transaction data and user behavior to detect fraudulent activities, such as unauthorized transactions or identity theft, reducing financial risks.

Biometric Authentication: AI-driven biometric solutions, such as facial recognition and fingerprint scanning, enhance security by providing secure and convenient user authentication methods.

Behavioral Biometrics: AI monitors users' behavioral patterns during transactions, detecting anomalies that could indicate unauthorized access or fraud.

Cybersecurity: AI algorithms identify and respond to cyber threats by analyzing network traffic for suspicious activities and vulnerabilities, bolstering protection against data breaches.

3. Risk Assessment and Management:

Credit Scoring: AI models assess creditworthiness by analyzing various data points, offering more accurate risk assessments for lenders and borrowers.

Portfolio Management: AI assists in creating diversified investment portfolios by analyzing risk tolerance, investment goals, and market conditions.

Loan Underwriting: AI automates the loan approval process by analyzing borrower data and determining creditworthiness, expediting loan decisions.

4. Personalized Financial Services:

Robo-Advisors: AI-powered robo-advisors offer personalized investment recommendations based on users' financial goals, risk tolerance, and market conditions.

Customer Insights: AI analyzes customer data to provide insights into spending habits, allowing banks and financial institutions to offer tailored services and products.

5. Regulatory Compliance:

AML (Anti-Money Laundering) and KYC (Know Your Customer): AI systems help in identifying suspicious activities and ensuring compliance with regulations by analyzing customer information and transaction data.

Regulatory Reporting: AI automates the process of generating reports required for regulatory compliance, reducing the risk of errors and ensuring accuracy.

Challenges and Considerations:

Despite the benefits, there are challenges in implementing AI in finance and fintech. These include concerns about data privacy, bias in AI algorithms, regulatory hurdles, and the need for transparency in algorithmic decision-making. Ensuring proper governance, robust security measures, and ethical use of AI are crucial for maintaining trust in these industries.

AI's impact on transactions and security in finance and fintech has led to increased efficiency, improved customer experiences, and enhanced risk management. As technology continues to evolve, these industries are likely to see even more innovative applications of AI in the coming years.

Chapter 4

Strategy and Implementation

Crafting an AI strategy aligned with business goals is essential to leverage the potential of AI technology effectively. **Most of these points have been stated before but they can be over emphasized.**

1. Define Business Goals:

Clearly outline your organization's short-term and long-term business goals. Determine how AI can help achieve these goals, whether it's improving operational efficiency, enhancing customer experience, increasing revenue, or entering new markets.

2. Identify AI Opportunities:

Identify areas within your business operations where AI can make a meaningful impact. This could include customer service, marketing, supply chain management, product development, risk assessment, etc.

3. Understand Data Requirements:

AI thrives on data. Identify the types of data necessary for AI implementation in your chosen areas. Determine whether you have access to the required data or need to collect and process it.

4. Assess Resources:

Evaluate your organization's existing AI capabilities and resources, including technical expertise, infrastructure, and budget. Determine whether you need to invest in talent or technology.

5. Set Key Performance Indicators (KPIs):

Define measurable KPIs that align with your business goals and reflect the impact of AI implementation. For example, improved customer satisfaction, reduced response times, increased revenue, or cost savings.

6. Develop a Roadmap:

Create a detailed plan outlining the phases of AI implementation. Prioritize projects based on their potential impact and complexity. Consider starting with smaller, achievable projects before tackling more complex ones.

7. Choose AI Technologies:

Select the AI technologies that best suit your objectives. This could include machine learning, natural language processing, computer vision, robotics, or a combination of these. Choose technologies that align with your data availability and business needs.

8. Data Preparation:

Clean, organize, and preprocess the data required for AI training and implementation. Data quality is crucial for the success of AI models.

9. Model Development and Testing:

Develop AI models using appropriate algorithms and techniques. Train and test the models using historical data, iteratively improving their accuracy and performance.

10. Integration and Implementation:

Integrate AI solutions into your existing systems and processes. Ensure seamless collaboration between AI systems and human resources to maximize efficiency.

11. Monitor and Refine:

Continuously monitor the performance of AI solutions and compare them against your defined KPIs. Regularly refine and update the models as new data becomes available.

12. Address Ethical and Regulatory Considerations:

Ensure that your AI strategy complies with ethical standards and relevant regulations. Address issues related to data privacy, bias, transparency, and accountability.

13. Employee Training and Change Management:

Train your employees to work effectively with AI technologies. Address any concerns they may have and communicate the benefits of AI in achieving business goals.

14. Measure and Communicate Success:

Regularly assess the impact of your AI strategy on achieving business goals. Communicate successes to stakeholders and adjust the strategy as needed based on results and changing business needs.

15. Continuous Learning and Adaptation:

AI is a rapidly evolving field. Stay updated on new developments and emerging AI trends. Continuously adapt your AI strategy to leverage new opportunities.

You can create an AI strategy that not only aligns with your business goals but also positions your company for growth, innovation, and competitive advantage.

Ethical considerations in AI are paramount to ensure that technological advancements are made responsibly and for the benefit of society as a whole. Balancing innovation with responsibility involves addressing several key ethical issues:

1. Bias and Fairness:

AI systems can inherit biases present in their training data, leading to discriminatory outcomes. It's important to identify and mitigate bias to ensure fair treatment and equal opportunities for all individuals, regardless of gender, race, or other factors.

2. Transparency and Explainability:

AI systems should be transparent, and their decisions should be explainable to users and stakeholders. This helps build trust and allows users to understand how decisions are being made, especially in critical applications like healthcare and finance.

3. Privacy and Data Protection:

AI relies on vast amounts of data, often personal and sensitive. Protecting user privacy and adhering to data protection regulations (such as GDPR) is crucial to prevent unauthorized access and misuse of personal information.

4. Accountability and Liability:

Determining who is accountable when AI systems make incorrect or harmful decisions can be challenging. Clear lines of responsibility and liability need to be established, especially when AI is used in critical domains like autonomous vehicles and healthcare.

5. Job Displacement and Socioeconomic Impact:

While AI can create new opportunities, it can also lead to job displacement in certain industries. Developing strategies for reskilling and upskilling workers affected by automation is essential to mitigate negative socioeconomic impacts.

6. Consent and Autonomy:

In cases where AI systems make decisions that affect individuals' lives, ensuring that users have informed consent and maintaining human autonomy over significant decisions is crucial.

7. Dual-Use Technology:

AI technologies can be used for both beneficial and harmful purposes. Ethical considerations include preventing the misuse of AI for malicious activities, such as deepfake generation or cyberattacks.

8. Algorithmic Accountability:

Organizations should be accountable for the algorithms they deploy. Regular auditing and monitoring of AI systems can help identify and rectify errors or biases that may emerge over time.

9. Global Implications:

Ethical considerations extend across borders. AI technologies should adhere to ethical standards regardless of geographic location and cultural differences.

10. Collaboration and Multi-Stakeholder Involvement:

Addressing ethical challenges requires collaboration among technology developers, policymakers, ethicists, and the public. Including diverse perspectives ensures a comprehensive approach to ethical AI development.

To balance innovation with responsibility, organizations should integrate ethical considerations into every stage of AI development, from data collection and model creation to deployment and ongoing monitoring. This involves creating multidisciplinary teams, conducting thorough impact assessments, and adhering to ethical guidelines and frameworks.

Ultimately, ethical AI not only safeguards against potential harm but also enhances trust, user adoption, and the long-term sustainability of AI technologies. It's a shared responsibility to shape AI in a way that benefits society while minimizing its risks.

Possible Challenges:

Data Availability and Quality: Insufficient or poor-quality data can hinder AI implementation. Ensuring clean, labeled, and relevant data is a significant challenge.

Algorithm Selection: Choosing the right algorithm for a specific problem can be complex. The algorithm's suitability for your data and problem domain is crucial for success.

Complexity and Integration: Integrating AI solutions into existing workflows and systems can be intricate. Ensuring seamless integration without disrupting operations is a challenge.

Resource Requirements: Implementing AI may require investing in skilled personnel, computational resources, and infrastructure. Resource constraints can impact the effectiveness of implementation.

Bias and Fairness: Bias in data or algorithms can lead to discriminatory outcomes. Mitigating bias and ensuring fairness is a critical ethical challenge.

Change Resistance: Employees might resist adopting new AI systems due to fears of job displacement or unfamiliarity. Change management and employee training are essential to address this challenge.

Regulatory and Legal Compliance: AI solutions must comply with industry-specific regulations and data protection laws, which can be complex and vary by region.

Measuring ROI: Determining the return on investment (ROI) of AI implementation can be challenging, especially when the benefits are indirect or long-term.

Unforeseen Challenges: AI implementation might reveal unexpected challenges or limitations that require adjustments to your strategy.

Rapid Technological Changes: The field of AI is rapidly evolving. Keeping up with new advancements and ensuring that your solutions remain relevant is a continuous challenge.

Chapter 5

Future Horizons: AI Trends and Beyond

The future of AI holds exciting possibilities across various domains. Here are some AI trends and developments to look forward to in the coming years:

1. **Explainable AI (XAI):** Ensuring transparency and interpretability of AI models will be crucial. XAI techniques aim to make AI decision-making understandable to humans, enhancing trust and accountability.

2. **AI Ethics and Regulation:** As AI becomes more integrated into our lives, governments and organizations will place greater emphasis on ethical considerations, leading to the development of regulations and guidelines to ensure responsible AI use.

3. **AI for Healthcare Breakthroughs:** AI will continue to accelerate drug discovery, personalize treatment plans, and assist in medical diagnostics. AI-driven genomics, disease prediction, and health monitoring will revolutionize patient care.

4. **Autonomous Systems:** Advances in robotics and AI will lead to more capable autonomous systems, ranging from self-driving cars and drones to industrial robots and smart appliances.

5. **Natural Language Processing (NLP) Advancements**: NLP will enable more natural and nuanced interactions between humans and machines. Translation, sentiment analysis, and chatbots will become more sophisticated.

6. **AI in Education:** AI-driven personalized learning platforms will adapt to individual student needs, improving education accessibility and outcomes. Virtual tutors and AI-powered assessments will become more common.

7. **AI in Climate and Sustainability:** AI will play a pivotal role in addressing environmental challenges by optimizing resource allocation, predicting natural disasters, and facilitating sustainable practices.

8. **AI-Generated Content and Creativity:** AI-generated art, music, literature, and other forms of content will become more prevalent, challenging traditional notions of creativity and intellectual property.

9. **Quantum Computing and AI Fusion:** The synergy between AI and quantum computing could revolutionize complex problem-solving by handling vast amounts of data and performing advanced computations.

10. **AI in Cybersecurity:** As cyber threats evolve, AI will play a critical role in detecting and responding to attacks, predicting vulnerabilities, and ensuring robust data protection.

11. **Human-Machine Collaboration:** AI will enhance human capabilities, leading to increased collaboration between humans and machines in fields like design, research, and decision-making.

12. **AI Democratization:** AI tools and platforms will become more accessible to non-experts, enabling individuals and smaller businesses to leverage AI capabilities for various applications.

13. **Edge AI:** Processing AI tasks directly on devices, known as edge AI, will reduce latency and enhance privacy by minimizing the need to transmit data to centralized servers.

14. **AI and Augmented Reality (AR):** The integration of AI with AR will create immersive experiences, improving real-time object recognition, and enhancing user interactions.

15. **AI in Agriculture:** AI-driven precision agriculture will optimize crop management, resource utilization, and yield prediction, contributing to sustainable food production.

16. **Neuromorphic Computing:** Inspired by the human brain, neuromorphic computing aims to build AI systems with energy-efficient, brain-like architectures, enabling advanced cognitive capabilities.

These trends indicate that AI will continue to shape and transform various industries, improving efficiency, decision-making, and innovation. While the future holds immense potential, it's essential to address ethical, social, and economic considerations to ensure that AI benefits society as a whole.

The Future Workforce: Navigating the Human-AI Collaboration

The evolving landscape of AI will inevitably impact the workforce, leading to a paradigm shift in how humans collaborate with AI systems. Here's how the future workforce might navigate the challenges and opportunities of human-AI collaboration:

1. Complementary Roles:

Rather than replacing jobs, AI is likely to augment human roles. AI can handle routine and data-intensive tasks, allowing humans to focus on complex decision-making, creativity, and emotional intelligence.

2. Skill Upgradation:

The workforce will need to continually acquire new skills to remain relevant. Skills such as data analysis, programming, critical thinking, and problem-solving will become even more important.

3. Reskilling and Upskilling:

Organizations will invest in reskilling and upskilling programs to prepare employees for AI integration. Continuous learning will be essential to adapt to changing job requirements.

4. Human-AI Collaboration:

Humans will work alongside AI systems, leveraging AI's strengths in data analysis and pattern recognition, while humans contribute context, empathy, ethics, and strategic thinking.

5. Creativity and Innovation:

As routine tasks are automated, humans can focus on creativity, innovation, and generating new ideas that drive business growth and differentiation.

6. Ethical Oversight:

Humans will play a crucial role in overseeing AI systems to ensure ethical decision-making. They will need to address potential biases, transparency, and accountability.

7. Hybrid Roles:

New roles that combine technical and human-centric skills will emerge. For instance, AI trainers, who teach AI systems and ensure their behavior aligns with human values.

8. Adaptive Work Environments:

Workplaces will adapt to accommodate AI-augmented roles. Tools and technologies that facilitate seamless collaboration between humans and AI will become essential.

9. Data Literacy:

An understanding of data and its implications will be crucial for employees in various roles. Data literacy will empower individuals to make informed decisions.

10. Lifelong Learning:

Lifelong learning will become a norm as individuals continuously update their skills to keep pace with technological advancements.

11. Emotional Intelligence:

Human skills like empathy, emotional intelligence, and interpersonal communication will be highly valued, especially in roles that involve direct human interaction.

12. Job Design and Flexibility:

Job roles might become more fluid and adaptable, allowing employees to switch between tasks that AI and humans are best suited for.

13. Innovation in Education:

Educational institutions will need to revamp curricula to prepare students for a future where AI skills and collaboration are crucial.

14. Human-Centric AI Design:

AI systems will need to be designed with user-friendliness in mind, enabling effective interaction and collaboration between humans and machines.

Chapter 6

Realizing Business Success in the AI Era

1. Healthcare: IBM Watson for Oncology

IBM Watson for Oncology uses AI to analyze vast amounts of medical literature and patient data to recommend personalized treatment options for cancer patients. It aids oncologists in making informed decisions, improving patient outcomes.

2. Finance: Ant Financial's Fraud Detection

Ant Financial, an affiliate of Alibaba Group, uses AI to detect fraudulent activities in real-time by analyzing transaction patterns and user behavior. This AI-driven approach has significantly reduced financial losses due to fraud.

3. Retail: Amazon Go Stores

Amazon Go stores use AI and computer vision to enable cashier-less shopping. Cameras and sensors track customers' movements and items they pick up, automatically charging their Amazon accounts upon exit.

4. Manufacturing: Siemens' Industrial AI Platform

Siemens developed an industrial AI platform that collects and analyzes data from manufacturing processes to predict maintenance needs and optimize production efficiency. This has led to reduced downtime and increased operational efficiency.

5. Transportation: Waymo's Self-Driving Cars

Waymo, a subsidiary of Alphabet (Google's parent company), has developed self-driving cars that use AI to navigate and make real-time decisions on the road. Their technology has logged millions of autonomous miles on public roads.

6. Agriculture: Blue River Technology's Weed Detection

Blue River Technology, acquired by John Deere, uses AI and computer vision to identify and target individual weeds in a field, allowing for precise herbicide application. This reduces chemical usage and improves crop yield.

7. Entertainment: Netflix's Recommendation System

Netflix employs AI algorithms to analyze user behavior and preferences, providing personalized recommendations for movies and TV shows. This AI-driven approach enhances user engagement and retention.

8. Energy: DeepMind's AI for Energy Efficiency

DeepMind, a subsidiary of Alphabet, uses AI to optimize Google's data centers, reducing energy consumption and cooling costs. Their AI algorithms manage the data center's efficiency and environmental impact.

9. Education: Carnegie Learning's AI Tutors

Carnegie Learning's AI-driven tutoring software analyzes student performance and provides personalized feedback and recommendations. This approach improves learning outcomes and helps educators tailor instruction.

10. Marketing: HubSpot's Content Strategy Tool

HubSpot's AI-powered tool uses natural language processing to analyze content trends and recommend topics for marketers. This streamlines content creation and improves content's relevance and effectiveness.

These case studies demonstrate the diverse applications of AI across industries, from healthcare and finance to retail and transportation. They highlight the transformative impact of AI on processes, customer experiences, and overall business outcomes.

Pitfalls to avoid

Learning from AI implementation failures is essential to avoid common pitfalls and ensure successful adoption. Here are some lessons from past failures:

1. Insufficient Data Quality and Quantity:

Lack of clean, diverse, and representative data can lead to poor AI performance. Ensure your data is of high quality, relevant, and sufficient for training accurate models.

2. Overlooking Ethical Considerations:

Ignoring ethical aspects such as bias, fairness, and privacy can lead to negative consequences. Incorporate ethical considerations from the start to build responsible AI solutions.

3. Lack of Clear Business Objectives:

Failing to align AI projects with clear business goals can result in directionless efforts. Define objectives, KPIs, and expected outcomes before starting any AI implementation.

4. Complexity Over Practicality:

Overcomplicating solutions with overly complex algorithms can hinder implementation. Prioritize practicality and simplicity to ensure smooth integration and adoption.

5. Underestimating Resource Requirements:

AI projects may require significant computational resources, skilled personnel, and time. Assess resource needs accurately to prevent delays and unexpected costs.

6. Neglecting Change Management:

Resistance to change from employees and stakeholders can undermine AI adoption. Prioritize change management, involve stakeholders early, and communicate the benefits clearly.

7. Ignoring Human-AI Collaboration:

Excluding humans from the loop or relying solely on AI can lead to errors. Focus on creating effective human-AI collaboration that leverages both strengths.

8. Failure to Continuously Update Models:

AI models need continuous training and updating to remain accurate. Neglecting regular updates can result in performance degradation over time.

9. Overhyping AI Capabilities:

Setting unrealistic expectations for AI's capabilities can lead to disappointment and distrust. Be transparent about AI's limitations and what it can realistically achieve.

10. Lack of Domain Expertise:

Developing AI solutions without involving domain experts can lead to inaccurate or irrelevant results. Collaborate closely with domain experts to ensure AI solutions address real-world challenges.

11. Poor Project Management:

Inadequate project planning, unclear roles, and lack of communication can derail AI projects. Implement effective project management practices to keep projects on track.

12. Not Validating with Real Users:

Failing to validate AI solutions with real users can result in products that do not meet user needs or expectations. Involve users in testing and validation stages.

13. Ignoring Feedback and Iteration:

Disregarding user feedback and failing to iterate based on insights can lead to suboptimal solutions. Embrace a feedback-driven approach for continuous improvement.

14. Overlooking Regulatory Compliance:

Neglecting regulatory requirements, such as data protection laws, can result in legal issues and financial penalties. Ensure AI solutions adhere to relevant regulations.

15. Technology for Technology's Sake:

Implementing AI without a clear business case or tangible benefits can lead to wasted resources. Ensure AI adoption is driven by business needs, not just the technology trend.

By learning from these pitfalls, organizations can make informed decisions, mitigate risks, and increase the chances of successful AI implementation that delivers tangible value.

Embracing the AI Revolution: Your Roadmap to Future Success

Embracing the AI revolution is of paramount importance in today's rapidly evolving technological landscape. Here are some key reasons why individuals and organizations should recognize the significance of AI and actively engage with it:

Competitive Advantage: AI can provide a significant competitive edge. Businesses that harness AI technologies can streamline operations, optimize decision-making processes, and offer innovative products and services, ultimately outperforming competitors.

Increased Efficiency: AI can automate repetitive and time-consuming tasks, freeing up human resources for more strategic and creative endeavors. This increased efficiency can lead to cost savings and improved productivity.

Data-Driven Insights: AI can analyze vast amounts of data quickly and accurately, uncovering insights that would be difficult or impossible for humans to discover. These insights can inform business strategies and drive better decision-making.

Personalization: AI enables businesses to provide highly personalized experiences to customers, tailoring products and services to individual preferences. This personalization can enhance customer satisfaction and loyalty.

Innovation: AI can accelerate innovation across industries. It empowers researchers, scientists, and engineers to develop new solutions and push the boundaries of what is possible in fields like healthcare, finance, and autonomous vehicles.

Cost Reduction: By automating tasks and processes, AI can lead to significant cost reductions in areas such as customer support, manufacturing, and supply chain management.

Societal Benefits: AI has the potential to address complex societal challenges, including healthcare diagnosis and treatment, climate change mitigation, and disaster response. Embracing AI can contribute to the betterment of society as a whole.

Job Creation: While AI may displace some jobs, it also creates new opportunities in fields related to AI development, data science, and AI ethics. Embracing AI can lead to a more diversified job market.

Global Relevance: AI is not limited to a single region or industry. It has global relevance and is being adopted by organizations worldwide. Staying ahead in the AI race ensures relevance on a global scale.

Future-Proofing: As AI continues to advance, it is becoming increasingly integrated into various aspects of our lives. Embracing AI today is a proactive approach to future-proofing your skills and your organization against technological disruptions.

In conclusion, embracing the AI revolution is essential for staying competitive, driving innovation, and addressing critical challenges in today's world. Whether you are an individual looking to enhance your skills or an organization seeking to thrive in the digital age, recognizing the importance of AI and actively engaging with it is a strategic imperative.

Enjoyed Our Book? Share Your Thoughts with the World!

Dear Unique Explorer

I hope this message finds you well, and I want to express my sincere gratitude for choosing to read my book, **"Navigating the AI Frontier"**. Your support means the world to me, and I'm thrilled that you've taken this journey with me through the pages of my work.

If you enjoyed reading **"Navigating the AI Frontier"** and found it valuable, I kindly request you to consider leaving a review on Amazon. Your review will not only be a great source of encouragement for me but will also help other potential readers discover the book.

Sharing your thoughts about the book, whether it's your favorite parts, what resonated with you, or how it may have positively impacted your life, can make a significant difference. Honest reviews from readers like you play a crucial role in the success of a book, and they serve as a guide for others seeking their next compelling read.

Here's how to leave a review on Amazon:

- ☐ Visit the Amazon website and log in to your Amazon account.
- ☐ Search for "[Your Book Title]" in the Amazon search bar.
- ☐ Click on the book's title to go to the book's page.
- ☐ Scroll down to the "Customer Reviews" section.
- ☐ Click the "Write a customer review" button.
- ☐ Share your thoughts, rating, and any insights you have about the book.
- ☐ Click "Submit" to post your review.

Your feedback is incredibly valuable to me, and it helps me improve as an author. Plus, it lets other readers know what they can expect from **"Navigating the AI Frontier."**

Once again, thank you for choosing to read my book, and I appreciate your support.

Wishing you many more wonderful adventures and blissful growth as you forge ahead with Ai evolution in your business!

Thank you!